BLAZE

poetry by Kahn Santori Davison

Willow Books, a division of Aquarius Press

Detroit, Michigan

BLAZE

Editor: Curtis L. Crisler
Cover art by Rodney Denne
Author photo by Kahn Santori Davison

ISBN 978-0-9961390-6-9
LCCN 2015945752

Credits
"Kortney" appears in *Barbaric Yawp* (2011).

"A Time Before Crack," "High," "Shhhhhh," "Impatiens," "Impatiens 2," "Emcee's Blues," "Uncle Frank's Funeral," "A Ride," & "Eminem Goes To School" appears in *Black Renaissance Noire* (2014).

Emerging Poets & Writers Series

Willow Books, a Division of Aquarius Press
PO Box 23096
Detroit, MI 48223
www.WillowLit.net

Printed in the United States of America

Dedication

For Wanda Davison, Oscar Davison, Robert R. Smith, and Coteal Smith.

Acknowledgments

Thank you to Vievee Francis and the group of Detroit poets formerly known as "Write Word-Write Now." There is no other way this could have happened. Thank you Latasha, Malachi, Makaiya, Jaylen, and Nyla for being the loves of my life.

Contents

INTRODUCTION

A Poetic Memoir

This story is closely based upon true events; they are facts framed by poetry.

BLAZE revolves around the experiences of a young man coming of age in Detroit. He is a child of the hip-hop generation—urban and world-wise. Like so many of his peers, he has experienced childhood traumas—while an infant, his mother died at his father's hands, then his father committed suicide two days later.

Raised by loving grandparents—a grandmother who raises plants, a grandfather who offers his insights—the boy experiences what many boys experience in high school: first love, lost love, sports, idolization of sports stars, and immersion in music during his journey toward selfhood. Like all teenagers, the boy is searching for a place for himself. He tries sports, love, music, then decides to rap and by extension, write. This decision enables him to express himself, to speak his truth.

BLAZE is divided into four stops along a journey to self-awareness. *Answers* (home/revelation/grief/push) covers the neighborhood, the caregivers/the grandparents, revelations about the deceased parents, wisdom gained from the grandparents, death of the grandparents, the death of other family members, and first love. *The Long Season* (school/body/search/struggle) covers sports, school, self-hood, the search for a place in the world, and the fight the search requires. *Days of Fame* (music/freedom/will/fire/defeat/questions of victory) covers hip-hop and growing up as part of the hip-hop generation, love/sex, and the need for self-expression. *Rock* closes out the collection and deals with his struggle to find acceptance for his new love: rock music, and covers some of his newfound heroes, including Detroit's own Jack White.

BLAZE is the story of one young man, yet it is a universal story as well, for we all must travel the road to self-discovery.

—KSD

A TIME BEFORE CRACK

After Jamel Shabazz

Watch the block get closed off.
Watch the balm of barbecue wake the neighborhood.
Watch the sun bake Jheri Curls into helmets.
Watch the open fire hydrant rinse the hot off necks.
Watch kids stand in line to slurp a humped stream from a garden hose.
Watch mouths of aunts and uncles dangle Newports and sip gin.
Watch mammas and papas when Junior drops the needle on Roberta Flack.
Watch youngsters when Junior drops the needle on Kurtis Blow.
Watch legs of wannabe b-boys, slinky on a sheet of cardboard.
Watch an emcee beg Junior for the mic like it's the last cup of red Kool-Aid.
Watch reefer pass behind backs like loose-leaf notes in a classroom.
Watch as the whole block   gets high.

HIGH

I thought Jordans and a gold chain was living it up.
—Nas

Grandma, with that same face she gave uncle
Robert when he needed somewhere to stay,
placed six crisp twenties in my palm for the
new Air Jordan's, the way aunt Sadie use to peel
off quarters for Ms. Pac Man. Within four minutes,
Randy was grinning on the front porch,
fingers suffocating a wad of greenbacks identical
to mine.   Destination   Northland Mall.
Where in thirty-minutes, Footlocker will
raise the roll-away gate to sixty high school
boys hoping to be picked up by whoever has *next,*
catch a rebound, or   the wink of a cheerleader.

PHOTO OF MY BEST FRIEND'S GRANDFATHER

His face was textured
like a perfectly crocheted quilt
that has spent a lifetime keeping
folks warm.

There's something about the way
his hair grays like the top half of an
ice cube. The way his eyes never blink
but speak with a defining silence.
The way wisdom resides in-between
the lines of his skin. The way
he stares at the lens, stoic,
motionless   but alive.

CHILDREN OF GROWN FOLK'S HIP-HOP ON FRIDAY NIGHTS

I felt like I was wearing a second layer of skin as
I walked through the cologne of fried chicken,
sweat, and Black & Milds.
Notorious B.I.G. pounded Pioneer speakers
so hard I thought he found a way
to fit his big butt inside the woofers.
It was the first time
me and Raven were allowed to be there.
Aunt Marie said,
"Y'all teens now, so no more watching cartoons in the bedroom."

Auntie Toya made us virgin daiquiris.
"Drink up babies."
It was our ghetto communion.
A heated game of dominoes was jumping off in the den,
the Knicks versus Rockets on the Zenith and
Uncle Earl and step-dad arguing over a
horseshoe game from last summer.

Someone switched the CD to Parliament's "Aqua Boogie"
Aunt Marie screamed, "Y'all taking me back now!"
Two lines formed as if there was a salute to Don Cornelius.
Aunt Marie pulled me and Raven to the line,
"This how we did it when we was y'all's age."
She hit the line first, her arms flung out,
went into some awkward swimming motion,
her booty shook as if she still wanted to remind
everybody that she still had a booty worth shaking.
Uncle Earl was next, tried to break dance
but had to be helped off the floor while
Auntie Toya sashayed down the line doing the Funky Chicken.
My turn was coming up, I gave Raven a nervous stare.
She smiled. Our rites of passage was near.

Shhhhhhh…

My grandparents forbade
anyone to talk about what happened
because things like that weren't supposed

to happen to good Christian-rooted families
like mine and when they did,
they were buried and burned with the cross-dressing

uncle, the incarcerated nephew,
and the love-child cousin. For nineteen years
everyone but me knew that my parents

weren't sacrificed to cancer or victims of a car accident.
My grandfather shushed my questions
like a toddler talking during church service.

My grandmother gave my inquiries
the same stare that made me swallow
my gum in Sunday school.

Other folks spoke of my mother with reverence
but didn't speak of my father at all.
That was the first clue,

but it was too dull. I wanted to believe
my parents were walking home from a blues show
when a mugger appeared, robbed, and shot

them both, and I would grow up bold, avenge
their deaths by becoming the incredible Batman.
That daydream lasted until I got to high school.

When grandmother passed during tenth grade with the secret
still clinched between her teeth,
it felt like any chance to find out what happened

departed with her. Four years would pass before
a newspaper article in an auburn chest
would tell me a gospel no one else could.

The comfort of not knowing what so many people did,
evaporated like holy water
on hell's doorstep. I closed my eyes and wept.

WANDA'S HOPE

1.
She massaged his shoulders and listened to the thoughts
he tried to hide   his coarse skin
never deterred her. She knew him.
She sat on his back
and swung at the demons.
She wished she could hide his skeletons. Saw how
they stalked him. Saw how hard he fought them off.
He rolled over, grabbed her fist.
It's in my blood, Wanda.
She slapped his face—
no, it's not.
His eyes closed,   fell
back into the emptiness
of his own world.

2.
While he slept, she took the test.
She took another, and another, and another.
She wanted to be sure.
A pigeon flew in the window, fell dead on the floor.
The eyes had been crushed.
She flung it out the window.

3.
He woke up, looked at her. It's morning.
No clock to punch.
She grabbed him.
"You love me.   I know you do.
We'll get it right, I make good money, we'll be okay,
you have your savings, you'll win, we'll laugh.
I have news for you, Oscar."

OBITUARY

Services were to be held today for Wanda Y. Davison, 29—
an oriole
a music teacher at Leslie Elementary School in Detroit
lush with song
police found her body in her home last Friday
limp as a dreary lyric,
and over the weekend discovered the body of her husband Oscar
lifeless
who police suspected of having fatally beaten her—
an unfinished lie resting on the tongue
investigators said he apparently committed suicide

CLEAN

Mrs. Little, a church member, remembers Wanda

Her mother buried her
in her wedding dress.
This bewildered most
but not me.
I remember when the double doors
of the sanctuary opened up
and I thought, "Good God from Zion,
that gal is clean!"
Mrs. Smith knew her and that fella
wasn't going to work out.
But I don't think she could
have seen *this* coming.
Hell, the boy cried forty days
and forty nights before he ever said I do.
I had the pleasure of seeing
little Ms. Wanda every week
in my Sunday school class.
Her black patent leather shoes,
white gloves,
always so clean.
That's how Mrs. Smith kept
her children.
Them white teeth smiled
every time I asked her a question,
'cause you know she was the smartest thing since King Solomon.
Oh yeah, I swear that gal was on the honor roll
every card-marking.
Mrs. Smith wasn't going to have it any other way.
And talk about playing some music,
a few Easters ago Ms. Wanda had that baby grand chirping so good
I thought Jesus himself would walk out that piano!
Mrs. Smith was so proud.
Then Wanda started messing with Iola's boy.
Mrs. Smith didn't take too kindly to that,
but I didn't see nothing really wrong with the fellow.

He was strong as Sampson,
complexion of Harry Belafonte,
and he carried his opinion like my Uncle Willie used to
carry his knife: sharp and quick on the draw.
Mrs. Smith wasn't impressed,
she felt her child deserved better.
I figured after Ms. Wanda brought her own beautiful child into the world
her mother's attitude would change—
it didn't.
I just don't think she felt that boy was clean enough for Ms. Wanda.
But that ain't nothing unusual,
I'd probably be the same
if I'd had a daughter.
But like my mammy used to say,
you gotta live your own life
and die with the consequences.
I asked Mrs. Smith was them papers correct
'cause it just don't seem possible for no man
to blow his own chest out with no shotgun.
She gave me a look that told me, "You'd betta
mind your own business,"
so I did.
Rumor said Ms. Wanda was thinking about
running off with some white collar fellow,
but I paid that hearsay no mind.
People love to gossip,
especially church folk.
I closed my eyes,
looked at Ms. Wanda one more time, said a prayer.
Sista Sharon worries for Ms. Wanda's little boy.
I don't.
He'll get raised just like his mama.

THE LAST DAYS OF OSCAR DAVISON

1.
He didn't mean to, you know?
But when she said she was unhappy
for the seventy-sixth time,
he snapped, panicked,
let the demons claim victory.
He had never hit Wanda before that day,
maybe that's why it only took one blow to kill her.
At first he tried to fool the Police—
he put me in the bathroom,
taped the door shut,
blew out the stove's pilots,
and let gas fill the house.
He watched from an abandoned house two days later
as a cop cradled me crying,
a coroner carried my mamma.
I hope they saw his
suicide note carved on the floor.
It's not all his fault,
God never should have let Mamma love him in the first place.

If the past is a compass to the future
then my bloodline seals my fate.

2.
My great-grandfather was an Irish bastard.
He had a four leaf clover tattooed on his chest,
a choleric temper in his fist, and
ten black slaves who worked till the owls spoke.
Midnight—
he would sneak into the barn,
rob the females of their spirit
and leave the devil's sin in their dreams.
The women gave birth to free men
who swung their penises with no conscience,
and acted on a conniption, no regard for regrets.

Wilbert preyed on church women.
Uncle Jacob got high off communion wine.
Uncle Zanny beat a man 'till he swallowed his own tongue.
My aunt thought it was some kind of curse
that infected all the men in our line.
Like vampires they came alive in the night,
and every time the sun rose,
they died little by little,
until there was nothing left
but empty whisky bottles,
bad memories,
dust.

3.
I wish Daddy could hold me —
envy my wife's smile.
He's thrown away that privilege.
His overalls bore Mamma's scent,
her skin is buried under his fingernails.
He muffled a sawed-off street-sweeper.
He stared inside the barrel,
it reminded him of space:
dark, inviting.
He closed his eyes,
gripped the steel,
mashed it to his heart,
fingered the trigger—
Tell the boys
I'm coming home.

WHAT I HATED MOST

were the comparisons.

Wanda was a straight "A" student. *Are you?*

Wanda was a fine piano player. *Are you?*

Wanda's shadow was an apple tree

that I fell too far from.

CLOSURE THROUGH A CARNATION

A Mother's Day tradition of wearing a red carnation to acknowledge your mother is living and a white carnation if she is deceased.

It was white, moist, like an egret after her egg has hatched.
Every Mother's Day it was placed over my heart,
attached to my lapel, secured with a stick pin
that would poke me if someone hugged me too tight.
Upon entering the sanctuary, eyes would grow, zoom,
open up my insecurity like a scalpel across my glands.
Even the ones who attended her burial would stare.
That used to mess with me   but no more.
Now, I peer at an old photo of myself, eleven months old
slumped in the backseat of a brown New Yorker,
a carnation clinging to the blue of my blazer
as if it knows it's our last time together.
I've seen this photo a million times, but, today is different,
I laugh out loud,
wonder why my parents would put me in a suit that's obviously two
sizes too big?
I raise the plastic flap of the scrapbook, nudge the photo
closer to the shots of my high school graduation and first grade t-ball game.

GARDENIAS

1.
Grandpa stands between a Redbud
and gardenias. He chortles into the aperture
as Aunt Elvin clicks the shutter.

Aunt Alice squints through the screen.
Grandpa pulls her to his side. Aunt Elvin
clicks the Canon again,

freezing their Colgate smiles
and the waxen gardenias beneath
a descending Winston-Salem
sun.

2.
Grandpa has come home to Winston to die.
He's on the fifth of a six-month expiry period
determined by a cancerous prostate.

The white cells are spreading, withering bones
like sulfuric acid corroding down the limbs of an elm.
One week to cessation, he collapses. My aunts, unaware

of his condition, rush him to emergency.
He's released, and my aunts care for him the way they did their moth-
er's
elderly years. Grandpa lives four more months.

3.
It's been five years since grandpa's last stutters.
The photo taken by Aunt Elvin is on her piano.
A clay pot of gardenias stands inches away.

She speaks of that day often—
the morning Grandpa arrived in Winston,
the hugs he gave away,

how you can repot a plant many times
but the roots will always find their way
back home.

IMPATIENS

For Coteal Smith

The last Saturday in April
Grandma beat the sun to the flower bed,
water-hose in one hand, trowel in the other.
She loosened up the winter-hardened dirt,
making seventy-two teacup-sized holes filled
slightly with water. Her pink palms—
moist and chilled from the morning dew—
held each flower the same way a child holds
a baby chicken after its egg has hatched.
Come here baby, help Grandma plant the Impatiens.
My five-year old eyes widened to the size of halogen bulbs
as grandma placed an Impatiens in my hand.
Be careful and do what I do, baby.
I watched her lay the flower in the hole, massage
the soil around the neck just like she did with Vicks
when my sinuses were stopped up.
I did the same. She smiled.

Four weeks to that day,
the seasoned bed was bustling with pinks,
purples, reds and whites.
Grandma pulled me close to her arthritic knees.
Soil is like the hands of God. You put something in it,
and it will grow.

IMPATIENS PT. 2

When the melanoma began to ascend
taller than her Impatiens could have ever grown,
I imagined them a bouquet of pinks, purples, reds
and whites spreading beautifully over Grandma's
defenseless body. I remember her casket being
lowered into the cooled soil, and wanting to help
the two men with shovels fill it up
and pat it down.

UNCLE FRANK'S FUNERAL

The only thing worse than the four angry women at Uncle Frank's
funeral were my girlfriends Jackie and Tamara
sitting tensely on opposite ends of the pew two rows behind me.
Before Mr. Pye cranked the casket closed, I eagle-eyed
his mortician's craftsmanship: Uncle Frank's high yellow
skin hardened to the color of a peeled peach as his
half-Irish grain of hair outlined his lips and chin
like an rhombus of dahlias. I needed my uncle to get up.
I needed advice to help me explain to Jackie and Tamara
that *lying* and *withholding information* were two
different things. But he laid stoic while the Pastor shushed
the quartet of women as they examined Uncle Frank's fibs and funds.
When the eulogy concluded the women stormed out
like four-year olds who just found out Santa was fake.
I rushed past Jackie and Tamara with the pallbearers, stared
straight, cupped my envious palms around the cold chrome bar.

URBAN DECAY 2

The old Packard Plant was our first
field trip in Mr. Dennison's photography
class. We all arrived armed:

tripods in hand, rolls of film
spilling out of cargo pants,
backpacks pressed against our spines,

brains confused, wondering why this
photography elective was so hard.
Mr. Dennison led us in this building that

hadn't birthed a car in over
thirty years. "This palace used
to produce one of the finest automobiles

ever made," he said as we walked down a
wide musty hallway stepping over sepia-
turned newspaper, discarded tires,

urine-smelling clothes and broken Zinfandel bottles.
A right, a left and four stairwells later
he stopped, aimed his lens at a peeling wall

bustling with graffiti. We cloned his actions.
"Eyesore to some, canvas to others."
A symphony of clicks ensued.

We continued to walk. We photographed an
old paint room, corroded cylinders, and
cardboard boxes made into someone's bed.

Mr. Dennison took us on several field trips that
semester. The Ford Model-T plant, Madison
Lenox Hotel, Michigan Central Train Station.

He loved the mystique, the bloom beneath the ruins. He spoke on each building's celebrated legacy passionately, as if we had nothing else to look forward to.

KORTNEY

Kortney was what high school fantasies were made of:
Kool-Aid colored eyes, vanilla pudding complexion,
hula-hoop sized earrings, skin-tight Calvin Klein jeans
with a belt buckle that said   H O T T I E.
She was a senior; I was a freshman, which meant
I'd have an easier time courting Halle Berry
than getting Kortney to give me a smile.
My English teacher, Ms. Folson, told me Kortney liked to write,
that I should share a few of my poems with her.
But my size 12 feet (I just grew into) and a heavy tongue
that made me sound like Zed from *Police Academy*
whenever I got too close to girls, wouldn't let that happen.
One Monday morning she stopped by my locker,
said Ms. Folson showed her the poem I wrote for my mother,
said she *liked* it, said it was *cool,* said she wanted to write poetry too.
I wanted to do the *Cabbage Patch* as if I had just won
the complete *Thundercats* action figure set.
From that day on, we exchanged smiles and waves
like Christmas gifts. Our connection was silent,
intimate as the daily nods I traded with the nameless neighbor,
the toddler that lip-synched me *Hi* as she walked to school,
the whisky-eyed vagrant who always offered me a toothless grin
as he extended his cup.

POSITIONING

Grandpa said life is all about positioning.
The energy between preparation and results.
If he was alive, he would tell you
the frailest man on earth can hit a Josh Gibson fastball
if he balances his feet, dips his tailbone,
stacks his grip and swings like there's a million dollars
hiding in the seams.

He told me the same went for meeting a good woman.
He said you gotta stay clean at all times because a
rainy day could put you in a cab next to your
future wife and the last thing a good gal wants to see
is man that wears his strikeouts like a crusty beard.

He loved to tell how he met my grandmother.
How a well-ironed suit, a southern smile and
the wrong bus was the seed to a 30 year union.
A black and white photo of them still rests
gently on his dresser. In it they're seated at a bar

holding hands while Grandpa flicks ashes
off a cigarette. *More cool than Bill Dee,* he used to say.
He loved to talk about the ole days—the marches,
the strikes, the juke joints, the first and second born—
every minute of life spent with my grandmother.

THE LONG SEASON

A POEM FOR PATRICE STRINGER WHO DUMPED ME FOR COREY "C-DOG" BUSBY BECAUSE HE HAD A CAR AND PLAYED FOOTBALL

1.
I hate you.

2.
When I saw you and Corey in the hallway
I ducked into Ms. Folson's classroom
and puked as if somebody had slipped
Castor Oil in my milkshake.

3.
I don't know why you like Corey.
The radio and speakers in his Neon
cost more than the car, he smells
like *Brut,* I heard he's the dumbest
kid in English class, and I saw
Coach Thompson telling
Chuck Winters that Corey always
fumbles.

4.
I hate you.

5.
I want back the herringbone
and the Mickey Mouse charm
I bought you for Christmas.
Maybe Corey will let you wear
his faded gold football helmet
charm hanging from that
dental-floss thin gold chain
he's so proud of.

6.
You're ugly anyway.
You smell like a kennel.
No wonder "C-Dog" likes you.

7.
You just wanna be like Marisa
and Chyna and have a boyfriend
on the football team. All ya'll
are faker than Corey's
"leather" 8-Ball jacket.

8.
Corey's probably Scrooge McDuck cheap.
I bet he even makes you buy your own popcorn
at the movies.

9.
If Corey is a "Dog"
that makes you his________.

10.
I hate you sooooooooo much.

11.
You're All I Need
was supposed to be our song.
We are the Dwayne Wayne and Whitley
of St. Martin Deporres High.
You said we were going to Homecoming together.
I had my grandfather buy me a new suit and everything.

12.
I miss you.

THE RIDE HOME FROM SCHOOL

Every day after school
Jaylen's brother picked us up.
Black sunglasses,
Raiders hat backwards,
never in a hurry.
His maroon '84 Monte Carlo
sparkled as if God
chewed up the sun and
spit flakes into the paint.
He parked two feet from the curb,
daring a sucka to hit it.
We tossed our bags in the trunk and
cruised off on spokes so perfect
I thought they'd been cleaned with dental floss.

Nothing felt cooler than
lounging in the backseat,
hot leather stinging my thighs,
12" woofer bass pounding my spine,
Dr. Dre and Snoop Dog
bum-rushing my eardrums.
Nothing felt freer
than gazing through the smoked tent,
the decayed school bricks,
the bus stop full of bullies,
athletes and girls.

NOT VERY BARRY

I told coach Huggins I was "da man" for the little league Cougars.
I told 'em Emmitt Smith was my distant cousin.
I told 'em I was a Ferrari in cleats.

OK Kahn, take the ball, hit the 2-hole, make a move on Busby here, and head down the field.

I took my three-point stance,
blew Busby a kiss,
bit down a grin in my mouthpiece,
eyeballed the pigskin,
Kevin yelled *Hike!*
I launched—
he tucked me the ball,
I hit the hole low,
Busby lunged,
I planted the right foot,
pushed off with the left,
did a 360,
left Busby hugging air,
but the right foot got stuck,
tangled with the left foot,
I fell down,
the ball came out,
Busby scooped it up
and ran the other way.

Kahn, get your behind down there with the defense!

I told 'em Bruce Smith would have a better chance snatching the boombox from Radio Raheem
than causing me to fumble.
I told 'em Dr. Octopus couldn't even tackle me inside the 20.

I never touched the football again.

NO GAME JERMAINE

Jermaine used to walk on the playground
the way Kobe enters the Staples Center.
A crisp white tee tucked in his
baggy red Nike shorts, Pirelli black
Air Jordan's shining like they were polished
with Armor All.
You would think Jermaine was the king of the court.

He wasn't.

Watching Jermaine play basketball
was like watching Charles Barkley figure skate.
One evening a new-jack showed up at the courts,
sized up Jermaine's swarthy six-four frame,
name brand apparel, and put him on his squad.
3 fouls and 5 air balls later the new-jack was up in
Jermaine's face, cussing, screaming and spitting.
Man, I would have been better off with Bushwick Bill
on my team. Jermaine replied with a push, the new-jack
swung back like C4 was in his fist, Jermaine ducked, countered
with a *Mike Tyson's Punch Out* uppercut that left the new-jack
laid out as Michael Spinks. Fifteen dropped jaws
circled around faster than a tipped row of dominoes.
Through the crowd's montage of "Ohs" and "Dangs" a voice rang—
I think you've found your calling, Jermaine!

A BLUE KAHN

After Terrance Hayes

If you believe in Karma—
than you can trace
your footsteps backwards

to the tack left on Angela Robinson's chair
in third grade, the penny candy stolen
from Ms. Jenkins's shop, and the first love

you told your first lies too. Everything
becomes relevant when you're
trying to Superman huff that black cloud

parked on your shoulder. When you're
trying to figure out which sins (you forgot
to ask forgiveness for) God has aimed back

at you with His pitcher's arm. Sometimes,
I would love to go back. I miss naïveté.
I miss the days when a bad grade, being cut

from the football team, were schoolboy blues
a Tupac CD and *In Living Color* reruns could fix.
A man don't know hard luck 'til his woman

has left his song homeless like a busted guitar
staring through a pawnshop window.
He don't know blues 'til he visits his parents'

grave, and finally comprehends that the only people
who loved him are gone
for good. That's the blues: a festering funk,

a stench, a song that hits your head like bird
droppings. So when them nasty notes get to falling,
Homeboy, you're in deep crap.

BALLAD FOR CHAKANA

Do you remember?...

The back stairwell,
the one under
Ms. Folsen's
math class,
our kissing spot
three minutes
before third hour—
tonguing—
the way L.L. showed
me in "I Need Love?"

I remember—
your Jordache jeans
tight like our
first time.
A Crayola marker
outlined your hand
on the back pocket
next to the mantra,
Don't touch.

I remember—
riding the cheese,
touching in the
back row,
that lovey-dovey stuff,
like we were
Treach and Pepa,
KC and Mary J,
grown.

I remember—the icebreaker.
Dancing? Not really.
More like screwing,

shaking it the
way cousin Curtis
did them dice.

I remember—
our last summer together,
the same year
EPMD broke up,
the same year
I fell in love with Quest.
You said, *Atlanta ain't that far,*
but I knew it was.
You cried, I wanted to,
but I held it in the way
my grandfather showed me.
I took off my African medallion,
place it around your neck,
because that's how the cats in
the movies did it.
"But they don't wear these anymore."
It don't matter.
It don't matter.

EMINEM GOES TO SCHOOL

Every Friday afternoon you can catch Champ
and Eminem at Osborne High
hustling cats like Wesley and Woody
in *White Men Can't Jump.*
40 bucks says nobody can
take the white boy!
Come on! Put ya money where ya rhymes at!
40 bucks says this pale faced Opie wannabe
will crush any kid that gets in his face.
6 minutes later, the hook reels in a tall,
doo rag-wearing sophomore who figures he
can take the easy 40 and buy his smiling girlfriend
the pair of K-Swiss she's been bugging him for.
Champ starts the break-beat, a crowd coils
and the sophomore cuts into Eminem's scrawny
stature, peeling Pumas, dingy white skin,
and the sewn-on Guess triangle attached to his no-name jeans.
But as the kid shoots a wink to his boastful girlfriend
and the crowd laughs, Champ brings the beat back.
Eminem stares him down like Marciano against Louis,
fires at the sophomore's fake Gucci chain,
the dirty gray sweater with leather patches (that he's wearing
on a 80 degree day), whack rhymes, dress socks with gym shoes
and his girlfriend's braces that resemble chrome railroad tracks.
The crowd hoots, hollers and then disperses.
Champ and Eminem split the 40, stop for burgers and fries,
then take the bus to Pershing High where school gets out in 10 minutes.

DAYS OF FAME

HIP-HOP, noun (hip-hop) or *hip hop*

1. A popular urban youth culture, closely associated with rap music and with the style and fashions of African-American inner-city residents *(The American Heritage® Dictionary of the English Language, Fourth Edition)*

2. Culture of urban youth that—**a.** tag their identities on brick walls **b.** spin, scratch, and blend records at high volumes simultaneously **c.** spit vulpine (sometime vulgar) rhymes that depict their environment **d.** move their limbs robotically, spin on heads, hands or buttocks and shake bodies in a seizure like motion *(Harlem Shake)*

3. The culture solely responsible for keeping pop culture abreast of contemporary slang. (Example: *fo' shizzle, fo' sheezy, bling bling, gettin' jiggy with it,* and *playa hater*)

SEARCHING FOR A GROOVE

I couldn't dance
I was born rigid
with splints on my legs
couldn't *Electric Boogie*
with puppet strings tied to my feet
couldn't *Running Man*
with pit bulls on my tail
I wanted to be Crazy Legs
spinning, kicking the sky like a falling helicopter
I was a wallflower,
couldn't even buy a dance from the bucktoothed girl with glasse
a black boy with no rhythm
no moves and no chance

ALL IN THE NAME

Everybody wanted
  to be Big Boi,
"so fresh, so clean"—
  a name on everything.
Donnie was
  a *Fila* man.
Kenny was
  Nike to the socks.
Gary had
  Girbaud for days.
I wanted *Nautica,*
  Pop shook "No."
Said, "the boat
  is a slave ship."
I pulled *Polo,*
  "No."
Said, "black folks
  don't play polo."
I grabbed *Tommy Hilfiger,*
  "No."
Said, "Hilfiger
  sounded like nigger."
Next day
  I came home with *Karl Kani.*
"The clerk
  said THESE are black-owned."
(And outta style).
I tried on my gear,
  plotted how
I was going
  to skip school.

FRIDAY NIGHT

After Q. Troupe

after ten
escape &
hope is
sought in
the DJ's
fingers

THE LIGHT

For DJ Slo-Poke

1MPC-2000 sampler
1Technics 1200 turntables
1Novation synthesizer
1U87 microphone
3 tablespoons of Bobby Caldwell's *When I Look in Your Eyes*

1.
Place the needle on the Caldwell LP
like liver on a plastic cutting board

2.
Snip out the chorus   Find 4 bars with
no vocals and chitlin' clean 'em,
then chop 'em off like frog legs
to be battered

3.
Loop the 4 bars, drain the bass
and stuff in a thicker, synthesized bass line

4.
Spread the 4 bars into 80 and plant the chorus
every 16

5.
Listen to the completed instrumental for 2 hours,
tweak it, till it, fiddle with it until it's tender

6.
Call Common
tell him to come over
step to the mic
and think about Erykah, hard

THE BLUE PROOF

After Terrance Hayes

Hey cuz, you weaker than the jaw on
Glass Joe. I see through you.

I'm the mayor of Detroit. Big baller.
Number one signal caller.

You're a whack rhyme addict.
Should've left ya raps in the attic.

They call me Illmatic.
The *Source* Unsigned Hype—I been that!

Blaze Battle—I won that!
Platinum Plus Sales—I done that!

I'm a Tropicana colored Benz dropped
down, while the windows in your Neon

won't even roll down. You still in diapers,
where ya wipes at? If you got skillz

then were ya album at?
I'm grey gators, Dobbs, pinstripes,

you're Pro Wings, Kross Kolors
and British Knights. I'm the juice.

Why you think they call me Proof?
I'm big dog on the mic, you just a hush puppy.

Yo' coward butt probably set me up,
paid ya mans to come into *Triple C*

and wet me up. It don't matter 'cause
I'm gonna run heaven like I ran Motown.

I even told JC *if one of ya*
boys steps to me, his butt is going down.

DREAMS OF THE MIC

For James Cagney at Cave Canem

It's unexplainable. I stroll off the stage with Jesus around my neck blinging women's contacts dry as if God pawned me the sun. They stare, pray I toss out one more drenched t-shirt, pray my sweat will cleanse them like the River Jordan, pray I can bless 'em, hold 'em *like I do the mic* when DJ Clue is gearing up the beat. Every now and then   I anoint one.

KARAOKE DREAMS

Before *Rick James _______!!*
There was me, every Wednesday night at Imonies looking for purpose through a white lettered thirteen-inch screen, a duck taped mic leaning on the carpeted stage freckled full of cigarette burns, Martell stains, and bad jokes. When Sherri called my name, every cat in the joint knew my song as I walked to the front high off strawberry daiquiris, a bad day, and chicken wings Sam left in the fryer too long. I gazed through the crowd with attitude like Miles at the 5 Spot, winked at Katrina and Salene, pointed to Dre and Randy to let them know they were going to be my Temps, and by mid-stream I was feeling it, like Ali vs. Foreman in the eight.

She's alright!
She's alright!
That girl's alright with me!
Yeahhhhhhh.
Hey, Hey, Hey, HEY!
She's a super freak, super freak!

And when the applause faded, I retreated back to my wobbly barstool, watered down daiquiri, drunk friends.

VIDEO GIRL

Any average dancer
can turn a few heads,

can reach inside a man
and snatch the libido

right out his crotch,
have him falling stank,

stuttering to the sand. This
alchemy began with Conga

drums, not 808s, not *Whistling*
while you twirk, not *Backing*

that thang up, not *Dropping*
it like it's hot.

The ancestors didn't intend for the magic
to be used like that, girl.

There's a sacred voodoo
language in those hips.

So priestess—
watch what you say, how you move.

HAIKUS FOR KIMBERLY JONES

1.
Junior Mafia!
The first album was so real.
Since then you've been fake.

2.
Them folks lied to you.
Your lips look like Ms. Piggy,
since those injections.

3.
You were in my dream.
Your implants jumped through the screen
and chased me away.

STUDIO GANGSTA

The fifth of Hennessy works its way around the studio
faster than Capri Suns at an elementary school recess. I sit

next to the lead emcee, Zeus, in a lopsided whicker chair in front
of the SSLJ-9000. "We gotta knock this song out in two

takes ya'll." Two other emcees pull out torn notebook paper,
flicker a blunt, walk behind the sound proof glass higher

than uncle Frank at my cousin's wedding. They gesture for me to
crank up their headphones, I cue them, they take off.

It's typical—women, rims, Rugers, and egos.
The younger boy: rustic yellow as old newspapers,

tries to spit so hard the vein in his neck is popping while his
corn-rowed, iced-out partner's tongue keeps failing him

in the middle of the ninth bar. "Take it back to *flossing*
big chips at the club." He's on his fourth take and Zeus

grows impatient as a landlord three months after the due date.
He looks at the uncertainty in the boy's eyes, at his baggy jeans

and hoodie costume covering his frail frame. Zeus clinches his fist,
stays quiet, and understands the reason his boy can't spit them lines.

STARS

Where do stars land after they fall?
Behind the pawnshop's bulletproof glass?
Inside decayed jewel cases?
At after-parties they hold onto their shine
like the last piece of glossy tape hugging their
portraits on high school lockers.

What dwells in their psyche as the light fades?
Suicide? 9 to 5? Mounting a comeback?

THE EMCEE

Most nights you didn't know if he
was gonna blaze the mic or not,
like a lighter that sometimes flickers,
and sometimes won't.
If his eyes were raining red from reefer,
the cognac on his tongue was kicking louder
than thirty-inch woofers,
then the crowd was going to get it!
Ol' Dirty Bastard   RAW!—
A spit shower, broken-English and break-beats.
But   if a sober evening ignited memories
of his father's rejection,
and the hoodie and Tims-wearing fans
in the front row reminded him
of the bullies from twelfth-grade
then the crowd's corn-rowed-platinum-hero
was gonna hit the stage petrified of his own shadow,
wilting   in the spotlight.

TECHNICS TYRONE

I shook my head in disbelief as Tyrone paid eleven grand for a pair of Technics SL1200 turntables his fingers were too clumsy to afford. Add that to his Tascam X9 mixer, Cerwin Vega speakers and you'd think Tyrone could keep a dance floor crammed like thief ants after a cornbread crumb is dropped. It didn't matter if he was spinning *Juvenile* w/ *Lil' John,* it sounded like 5 different radios blaring at the same time. He had about as much Jam Master Jay in him as Bobby Brown has Luther Vandross. Even DJ Polo tried to teach those heavy fingertips how to drop the needle on the hook like a tender nurse who spots the vein, how to change sleeves faster than Bruce Wayne, start and stop the breakdown like an Ella *scat.* But Tyrone was hopeless. His neighbors wouldn't let him DJ his own street's block party. I guess Granddaddy was right: *It don't matter the tools if the mechanic can't fix nothin'.*

EMCEE'S BLUES

How you gon' tell a boy
Whose daddy got locked up
While his mama rocked him
To sleep to Nina Simone
He can't rhyme?

How you gon' tell him
He can't hold the mic,
As if his ebonics
Is any worse
Than yours.

How you gon'
Call his music devil's music?
Take his blues away,
Like when grand-mamma
Snatched our Bird album off
The phonograph.

Negro please!
Have you ever listened
To the pictures he paints,
As if he's Jacob Lawrence
On the mic stand?
The drive-bys—the carjackings—
The pimps—the bitches—
The crack—the reefer—
The dollar-dollar-bill.

Give that boy his mic back!
Let him piss off some folks,
Shake up the world,
Spit   his blues.

EMCEE'S BLUES 2

Ain't you? Oh my God!
You was the illest mannn. Yo mannn, the first joint was Hot!
What happened to the second joint mannn?

I know you gon' come out with some mo' joints *mannn.*
My hand dove to my bag,
ripped out a picture from an old *Source* for him to sign.

In it, he's hoisting a platinum plaque
the way a 1st grader holds his first "A" while a gold Jesus face
with diamonds in the eyes and mouth

hangs loosely off his shirtless, tattooed body.
Sweat from par lights cooked his face.
I remember that night well—

the drenched white t-shirts
Bazooka launched into a sea of mouths screaming his name.
He misses it the way a preacher

misses his congregation after a sabbatical.
I miss the smile of a new woman
eyeing me as if I was Michael Jordan.

I miss the schoolboy blues
from eighth graders telling me, "Yo, I lost my mamma too,
Yo, I had to hustle in the streets too."

I miss hearing my life blasted through car speakers
over Al Green samples.
He misses the good music, a pack of squares, a gallon of Tanqueray

and a twelve-hour studio
session can make. But more than anything,
He misses being somebody.

He wants to tell me that his new joint is dropping this fall.
But he can't.   He can only sign the picture.
And pray the scent of album sleeves finds him again.

A RIDE

After Major Jackson

Who cares if you don't like
Jamall's 2005 Escalade: Pearl-colored,
midnight hued windows, spinning
rims talking in super-speed Morse code

hypnotizing shorty's eyes
like a ten-foot chrome metronome.
When the speakers fall to a murmur
and the passenger side window drops

he ain't gotta ask for a number,
cause shorty already wanna ride.
Wanna be on the air conditioned side of the tint
hugged in pimped-out beige leather

as if she's in Saks trying on a coat
she know she can't afford.
Jamall licks his lips, smirks,
switches the CD to R. Kelly

just to make sure that shorty knows the fare.
Her Lil' Kim video moment is near,
Jamall thanks God for his ride,
shorty waves at you, reclines, smiles.

A RIDE PT. 2

Jamall presses the left blinker, glides right fingertips down shorty's
thighs the same way a painter rubs and primes his drywall.

Shorty shoots a sly wink to let him know that she approves, but before
the light can flick green, an 81 El Dog buts burgundy on the back

of his ivory Escalade. Jamall flings his arms upward, drops them—
the universal sign for, "Awlllll s%#t." A man of similar

dimensions plus thirty years steps out, eyes both bumpers.
Man I thought you was moving, I swear I did.

Jamall studies the flaked paint, sagging tailpipe, corroded chrome
on the old-timer's Caddy, and figures he ain't got no insurance.

The old cat crosses eyes with shorty in the passenger-side mirror, sends
a humble smile. *Take my number captain, Imma get it fixed, I got money.*

Jamall climbs back into his ride, heavy-foots the gas, trying to outrun
shorty's second thoughts and the decaying image of the old timer's grill.

KRS-ONE LIVE IN DETROIT, DECEMBER 17TH 2004

To understand why this cat is so bad
you gotta study the way
he holds the mic,
rapacious, like a pole vaulter
on takeoff.

The harder the ginger-colored stage lights
fry the sweat over his brows
the more he loves it, gets into it
like Jack Johnson in the fifteenth
versus some white boy.

Take 'em to school KRS!
The boroughs, the Bronx,
the bridge where raw lyrics
jump through woofers the way
L.T. busts through blockers.

Where them bling-bling newbies at?
Them sagging pants cats who think
emceeing is about posting up,
clutching your crotch like somebody's
trying to hit you in the damn balls.

Rock the crowd KRS!
Show 'em ya tongue is still sharper
than a butterfly blade in a street fight.
Show 'em how twenty years of marinated
rhymes taste like leftover soul food,
reheated   to perfection.

AUNTIE SADIE GOES TO THE JAY-Z CONCERT

When Auntie Sadie wanted to come with me
to the Jay-Z concert I was nervous,
like a fourth grader when his mother tells
the teacher she's going to sit in on the next class.
Ba-by don't worry, I won't be in your way.
I pulled in her driveway Friday evening,
she came out in the blue jean dress I bought
her last Mother's Day. Her freshly braided
gray hair was slightly shining
like the top halves of ice cubes. We talked
like never before, she said, *Suge killed Biggie,*
Russell Simmons is a crook and
50 Cent is overrated. I laughed.
She reminded me of my teen years regurgitating
opinions from ESPN at the barbershop.
We pulled into the arena, parked, found our seats
as a local group was finishing their set.
Auntie reached in her purse, shot me a twenty—
Get me nachos, Snickers and a half-cup of Coke.
When I returned, she pulled out a small flask,
poured half the contents in the cup. My mouth
fell as if I had just witnessed Mother Mary smoke
a joint. *What's wrong, you don't drink Crown Royal?*

THE LAST DAYS OF DILLA 1974-2006

For Versiz

J Dilla heads
into his bedroom studio
with a new set of headphones
and a crate full of classics.

He sits at a sand-colored table,
moves fingers feverishly
between turntable and drum machine,
creating a communion of baselines

and horn samples.
More music than life left.
3 hours, 1 bottled water, an aspirin later—
a song is born.

A WORLD WITHOUT HIP-HOP

No Run DMC
No Kurtis Blow
No DJ Kool Herc
No Afrika Bambaataa
No Crazy Legs
No Tracy 168

No
Yes-Yes-Ya'll
No
Throw ya' hands
in the airrrrrrrrrr —
wave
'em like ya' just
don't carrrrrrrrre—
No
ALL THE UGLY PEOPLE BE QUIIIIEEETTT

No
Niggaz 4 Life
Public Enemy
2 Live Crew
Death Row

NO PARENTIAL ADVISORY

No
Ice Cube
Ice-T

No
Flavor Unit
Flavor Flav

NO LIL' MO, LIL' WAYNE, LIL' FLIP, LIL' BOW WOW, LIL' KIM, LIL' JOHN

NO Parachute Pants
NO Gold Ropes
NO Polka Dots
NO LL Cool J Troops
NO Gucci Links
NO Air Brushed Levis
NO Fake Versace
NO Jesus Pieces
NO NAME BRANDS

No
Krush Groove
No
Do The Right Thing
No
Beat Street
No
Hype Williams
No
F. Gary Gray
No
Eminem
No
Will Smith

No Budweiser Super Fest
No Russell Simmons
No Sprite Commercials
No Hard Knock Life Tour
No Gold
No Platinum

NO
Black
on Both Sides
NO
Vote or
Die

NO
X-Clan

No
RUKUS

NO
LOUD

NO
LIFE

THE DAY HIP-HOP STOPPED BY BAKER'S KEYBOARD LOUNGE

After Thomas Sayers Ellis

A helluva collection: poets, balladeers,
Rappers, musicians. Juice like that
Ain't been in Baker's since Cannonball,
Don and Joe Hunter broke notes together.
You can hear jaws dropping all the
Way to the south side of heaven:
Where halos rest at a tilt and the bar
Never sleeps. Cats been waiting on
This for a long time. Here, there is no velvet rope,
No judgment. Every 20 minutes, a new jack
Takes the mic, pants sagging, saliva flying,
As a legend on keys combs back his waves,
A rookie with a pic in his 'fro warms up the snare,
A veteran trades his square-holder for an alto. Smell it,
Taste it, smell it, taste it, smell it, taste it, smell it—
The stuff that 60 years and 7 generations has produced.
Funk like this don't congregate too often—
Somebody crack a window.

HOW TO BATTLE RAP

For the Emcees at the Hip-Hop Shop, 1994

You gotta step to the mic a predator—
like a gray wolf after the sun has dipped.

When Dilla drops that needle, and Proof
gives you the nod: you got 90 seconds.

The opposite side of you is the weakest
rapper that ever picked up a microphone,

so you gotta cut into his bald-headed momma
and his 1964 Easter suit-wearing daddy.

And when it's his turn—
stare him down. Drown him in your gaze.

Make him go blank, drop the mic
and walk offstage. Do this, and maybe

some local label will give you a shot,
promise to make you a star, chew on your popularity,

laugh in ya face, and dare ya to walk away.

THE LAST WORDS OF JAZZ

So here I am
broken into a million pieces
as a shattered Rubik's Cube.
It wasn't supposed to end like this.
I was Jazz man.
An Autobot,
a Transformer,
a movie star,

I was Jazzzzzzzzzzzzzzzz baby!

Spielberg promised me a sequel,
auto shows, *DUB* covers,
my own line of tires.
That backstabber even said
he would put in a good word
for me to the new Knight Rider.
All that was before he let Megatron
rip me in half. Yo Speilberg:
THAT WASN'T IN THE SCRIPT!
They must've found out I was black.
Too much slick slang on my part
gave it away. But hell, I can't help it
if I was cooler than everybody else.
But that's show business, I had my 15 minutes.
If anybody needs me for a cameo I'll be
in the scrapheap with Big Foot, the GoBots,
and Herbie Love Bug wannabes.

Dear Patrice,

When I die, leave my notebooks in the garage. Don't show nobody them old poems. Don't nobody wanna read about Uncle Willie's fat white mistress (besides, I promised him I wasn't going to publish those anyway), or Great-Grandma's shotgun, Cousin Carl's herpes and Aunt Elma's gastritis that showed its ugly face at her own wedding. Whatever you do baby, don't tell them folks about my journals in the attic. Those men are ruthless baby, please don't. They'll take the poems about my mamma and make a Master P remix. They'll have Busta Rhymes in the poems I wrote about Granddaddy's funeral. You gotta listen to me baby, because those men just don't care. They'll offer you money, but don't worry, I got a stash for you at a bank in D.C. Just don't give them men my poems baby. Just don't give them men my poems.

ROCK

AIR GUITAR

Nothing makes sense about
A nineteen year-old black kid
Finding fantasy in a bedroom mirror
Pressing wind into make-believe sound

A nineteen year-old black kid
Hiding from hood and homeboys
In baggy jeans and Jordans
With an Ice Cube bandanna tight

Hiding from hood and homeboys
He turns his Discman from high to heavy
Takes foxy lady down, then back up
One-hops it across a tired rug

He turns his Discman from high to heavy
Locks the door to guard his daydream
Shuts his eyes until he sees the stage
Grips the strat like it's his woman's tit

Locks the door to guard his daydream
This is before *Guitar Hero, Rockband*
When shoe contracts and BET
Told black boys who their heroes were.

Before *Guitar Hero, Rockband* when
Playing a guitar wasn't about scoring points
When the weight of stereotypes and confusion made
Guitars too heavy for most black boys to play.

DISCOVERING

I didn't know black boys had guitars,
thought God made all rock stars
white.
Your paisley bandanna,
dancing between sweat and light.
Tight fuchsia leather pants,
medallion pounding
against flesh and whole notes.

Your story—
best told in licks and chops,
out the cry of an amplifier,
in the soggy blues of your baritone.

I remember the day I found you,
snug dusty between Miles and Lennon.
I put needle to song.
The popcorn and electricity wailing
through the Pioneers.

PROFESSOR OF SOUND

This night
Jimi is testing noise

as if he's an engineer,
as if he's Ben Burtt,

as if he's James Allen Hendrix,
professor of sound at Seattle University.

Remembering
the bellow of a '64 Chrysler,

the way the wind pulled into manifold,
unfolding through exhaust, leaving its score on the world,

the alley cat's nightly screech
forcing the neighborhood to listen,

Brenda dragging nails across a black chalkboard,
how she loved the attention, relishing in the cringes and scowls.

When his eyes open, blurry, he can hear
the citrus sweet sound of his mother's kiss,

his face wrapped in her bosom,
the sound of her memories.

INTERVIEW WITH AMP FIDDLER

Amp opened the door to his eastside bungalow buzzing with sound and smell. A TV surrounded by 3 youths smothered in white T-shirts, 2 tattooed women in the kitchen frying wings between exchanges of Newports and man talk. My editor told me Amp Fiddler is really big overseas, which translated to Amp Fiddler is nobody here. I followed Amp down the rocky stairway to a basement soaked with LPs, tapes, and empty beer cans. Amp talked how his brand of soul/funk was selling in London like iPods, but in the States like typewriters. How he could make a French woman's panties dissolve by playing a 10-minute drum solo. How him and Slum Village got more handclaps in the U.K. than a black Easter service. We talked Muddy Waters, James Baldwin, Derek May, and Jimi Hendrix. We talked album sales, tour dates and his background. How ever since he was a kid, he's always had to beg his family to come see him perform.

DJ SAM "THE SENSATION" BOOKER SPEAKS ON JIMI

Only thing black about that negro
was his daddy. Not his clothes,
not his music, not his dope.
You ever seen a Harlem brotha
dressed up in some mess like
that? You ever hear George
Benson playing some mess like
that? I gave 'em a chance, went to
his show and can honestly say I'd
rather watch monkeys throw shit
at each other. Black folks need to
stick to black music. It's a shame
how he died, laying up there,
throat full of throw-up, some
white girl there with no clue
what to do.

LINER NOTES

Mixed, produced and arranged—Jimi Hendrix
Electric guitar, vocals, piano, percussion—Jimi Hendrix
A barbed blade redefining sound—Jimi Hendrix
Funky cowboy, bluesman, psychedelic crooner—Jimi Hendrix
Played yo life story with 3 rubber bands and a toothpick—Jimi Hendrix
Burnt orange, fuchsia, and fluorescent—Jimi Hendrix
Founder of the amplifier graveyard—Jimi Hendrix
Electricity, sweat, and lysergide—Jimi Hendrix
Fire, Foxy Lady, Freedom and Farwell—Jimi Hendrix

JACK WHITE

It's one of those headlines you don't expect to read.
"Jack White Brawls with Fellow Garage Rocker at Detroit Club."
Rockers not rappers? Who knew the big axel had rockers?
Unless you want to count Kid Rock, but no one ever
wants to count Kid Rock. Who is Jack White? How come
there's a white boy in my city beating down cats like
Tommy Hearns that I don't know about? I mean Jack White
left dude's face looking like a *MAD* magazine cover.
I wonder what made Jack White go Bill Laimbeer on him?
What made him trade his timber for this man's blood?
What Detroit blues was running from his pores as he pounded
knuckles against flesh? What images of this stubborn city
did Jack White see as he watched the broken blood vessels
circle dude's eye, caving in slowly.

The White Stripes at The Masonic Temple October 1, 2005

On a cold & navy
night   Jack—
dressed in
superhero red
pants—is
slapping around
half notes
as if his
guitar was a
cricket bat.

In this black &
brown town where
woofers submerged
in rusty trunks   fill
the glow of streetlamps
with 808 bass   Jack
is back on
Hastings   back
in his room
whaling   into
the a.m.
into fable.

Within this arched
sanctuary   known
for symbolism &
fraternity   Jack
is restoring history
raking pick against self
against city
against us.

Q&A WITH JACK WHITE OF THE WHITE STRIPES

What kind of band is the White Stripes?
We're fiddlers, spoon-tappers, harmonicists,
a blues duo cloaked in rust and desire.

Like garage rock right?
Garages are for jalopies and sports cars.

What drives your creativity?
Creativity is best when opportunities are less like
a blind man exploring his somberness through
a two-string banjo and a toe-tap.

How would you describe a White Stripes show?
Like joy riding in a brand new Mustang only to find
out the Mustang is a 1957 Ford pick-up.

Do people ever compare you to Kid Rock or Eminem?
Do people ever compare you to Al Roker or Stewart Scott?

Why did you leave Detroit?
When covetousness rears its head like a snake
after the mouse is dropped,
the music can't be born,
and when the music can't be born—
you leave.

POST DREAMS

I'm 35 years-old
staring at history
through Youtube—
a used Gibson
in palm playing
"Mannish Boy"
with Muddy.
My wife's confused,
thinks I'm crazy,
says Muddy would
slap the shit
out of me if
he heard me
slaughtering
his hymn.
She's worried
I'm ditched in a
premature mid-life
crisis—trying to
channel the inner
guitar god
I never became.
She's right
(about god and Muddy).
I explain this
guitar is like
our first born—
I didn't know what
to do the first time
I held him but
I knew it felt right.
And when she
falls asleep
I'm going to
take Gibson
back to my old 'hood—

post up under the moon,
strum "Mannish Boy"
'til my fingers feel
like gummy worms,
'til I'm ducking
beer bottles.

ROCKSTAR

For Latasha Davison

This is the poem where I
revisit our initial collision.
The poem where I remind
you how star-struck you
were as I exited the stage
sweaty, guitar strapped
to my back like a surfboard,
how you lip-synced me
your number, and when I
offered to take you to
breakfast after the next
night's show, you declined.
Said after show dates were
for groupies and one night
stands. So you dropped
your life like bad cabbage
and joined me in Alberta,
where we studied cardiology
on each other. I sung
you ballads in Quebec,
proposed in Nova Scotia,
and promised I would
place every province
in your hands.
But every time I tell this
story to strangers you burst
into laughter at the
lip sync part because
we've never been further
than Toronto and I can
play a guitar as well
as I can do open heart surgery.
And I know you wondered
what was going through
my cerebrum when I borrowed

mortgage money for a Les Paul,
but lately I think you've been
looking at me and seeing
Ward Cleaver when I want you
to see Slash. I know Mike Brady
was a good father but I have
a feeling you'd rather
go to bed with Lenny Kravitz.
I want to be your rockstar
your fireworks, sprayed
champagne, your zero to sixty
in five seconds, prescription
for Oxycodone, coffee
in the a.m. I want you
crying for no reason, fainting
like girls at Michael Jackson
concerts. I want my poster
on your walls, my bumper
sticker on your butt. I want you
asking for my autograph
every morning and throwing bras
and panties at me when I come
home from work. So one
night, when you catch me
searching for resolve in the dissonant
strings of my guitar, when I'm in
the mirror like a child playing pretend,
I'm just waiting to see your sandalwood
colored reflection behind me, waiting for
you to show me you're my number one fan.

About the Author

Kahn Santori Davison is from Detroit, Michigan. He is a 2015 Kresge Fellow. Formerly an arts columnist for *The Gazette News* and Arts and Entertainment writer for the *Michigan Citizen*, he is currently a music writer for the *MetroTimes* and editor for AUXmedia. A graduate of Oakland University, Kahn has served as a creative writing instructor at Detroit Impact Community Center and for the Inside Out Literary Project. He was one-half of the poetry group Khaos and co-starred in the award-winning play *Mahogany Dreams.* Kahn has been featured on countless radio and TV shows. A Cave Canem fellow whose works have been featured in *The Alabama Poetry Society, The Entoitist, The Baltimore Review,* London's *X-Bout, Barbaric Yap, Callaloo, Black Reniaissance Noire* and *The Litchfield Review,* Kahn has read and lectured across the U.S., in Canada and in Europe. In addition to being the owner of Kahn Santori Photography and Primal Immortality Art and Shirts, Kahn is a proud husband and father of four.

www.ingramcontent.com/pod-product-compliance
Ingram Content Group UK Ltd.
Pitfield, Milton Keynes, MK11 3LW, UK
UKHW040556210726
13854UKWH00007B/813